Passengers Once More
New and reopened stations
and lines since 1948

WALES, THE BORDER COUNTIES
and MERSEYSIDE

Cwmbach is typical of several smaller stations reopened in South Wales over the last decade.

Passengers Once More
New and reopened stations
and lines since 1948

WALES, THE BORDER COUNTIES
and MERSEYSIDE

John Hillmer

Silver Link Publishing Ltd

First published in 2011

British Library Cataloguing in Publication Data

A catalogue record for this book is available
from the British Library.

ISBN 978 1 85895 357 3

Silver Link Publishing Ltd
The Trundle
Ringstead Road
Great Addington
Kettering
Northants NN14 4BW

Tel/Fax: 01536 330588
email: sales@nostalgiacollection.com
Website: www.nostalgiacollection.com

Printed and bound in the Czech Republic

Abbreviations

ATW	Arriva Trains Wales
BR	British Railways
BRC	Barry Railway Centre
CLC	Cheshire Lines Committee
CR	Cambrian Railways
DFR	Dean Forest Railway
EC	European Commission
EEC	European Economic Community
EMT	East Midlands Trains
ERDF	European Regional Development Fund
EWS	English Welsh & Scottish Railway
FNW	First North Western
FTPE	First Transpennine Express
GCR	Great Central Railway
GwilR	Gwili Railway
GWR	Great Western Railway
HST	High Speed Train
LM	London Midland
LNWR	London & North Western Railway
LlanR	Llangollen Railway
NR	Network Rail
PBR	Pontypool & Blaenavon Railway
PRNI	Project of Regional and National Importance
PTE	Passenger Transport Executive
RR	Regional Railways
RSBR	Rhondda & Swansea Bay Railway
SVR	Severn Valley Railway
SWR	South Wales Railway
SWJR	Severn & Wye Joint Railway
TSR	Telford Steam Railway
TVR	Taff Vale Railway
VGR	Vale of Glamorgan Railway
W&S	Wrexham & Shropshire

Contents

Bibliography

Baker, S. K. *Rail Atlas Great Britain & Ireland*, 12th ed
    (OPC, an imprint of Ian Allan Publishing, 2010; ISBN 978 0 86093 632 9)
Bridge, M. *Railway Track Diagrams, No 3 Western*
    (TRACKmaps, 2010; ISBN 9780 9549866 6 7)
Butcher, Alan C. *Railways Restored*
    (Ian Allan Publishing Ltd, ISBN 0 7110 3216 5)
Gatehouse, Don and Dowling, Geoff *British Railways Past & Present*
    No 26: South Wales Part 1 (Past & Present Publishing Ltd; ISBN 1 85895 082 1)
    No 28: South Wales Part 2 (Past & Present Publishing Ltd, 1995; ISBN 1 85895 084 8)
Gough, Terry *British Railways Past & Present*
    No 37: South Wales Part 3 (Past & Present Publishing Ltd, 2002; ISBN 1 85895 162 3)
    No 38: West Wales (Past & Present Publishing Ltd, 2002; ISBN 1 85895 175 5)
Hillmer, John *Gazetteer of the Railways of Wales: A photographic record of the British Rail*
    network at privatisation (Silver Link Publishing Ltd, 2008; ISBN 978 1 85794 303 0)
Hillmer, John and Shannon, Paul *Past & Present Companion: The Great Western in North*
    Wales (Past & Present Publishing Ltd, 2007; ISBN 978 1 85895 255 0)
Hopkins, Danny *The Inside Guide to the Steam Railways of Britain*
    (the publishers of *Steam Railway*, 2010; no ISBN)
Jacobs, Gerald (ed) *Railway Track Diagrams, No 4 Midlands & North West*
    (TRACKmaps, 2005; ISBN 0 9549866 0 1)
Quick, Michael *Railway Passenger Stations in Great Britain: a Chronology*, 4th ed
    (Railway & Canal Historical Society, 2009; ISBN 978 0 901461 57 5)
Rail Times for Great Britain, May-December 2011
    (Middleton Press; ISBN 978 1 906008 994
Shannon, Paul and Hillmer, John *British Railways Past & Present No 36: North Wales Part 2*
    (Past & Present Publishing Ltd, 2007; ISBN 978 1 85895 163 8)
    No 39: Liverpool and Wirral
    (Past & Present Publishing Ltd, 2002; ISBN 1 85895 199 2)
Siviter, Roger *Past & Present Companion: The Central Wales Line*
    (Past & Present Publishing Ltd, 1999; ISBN 1 85895 138 0)
    Past & Present Special: The Severn Valley Railway
    (Past & Present Publishing Ltd, 1995; ISBN 1 85895 080 5)
    Past & Present Companion: The Severn Valley Railway
    (Past & Present Publishing Ltd, 2008; ISBN 978 1 85895 145 4)
    British Railways Past & Present No 32: Mid Wales and the Marches
    (Past & Present Publishing Ltd, 1998; ISBN 1 85895 137 2)
Stretton, John *Past & Present Companion: The Dean Forest Railway Volume 1*
    (Past & Present Publishing Ltd, 2006; ISBN 1 85895 206 9)
    Past & Present Companion: The Dean Forest Railway Volume 2
    (Past & Present Publishing Ltd, 2007; ISBN 978 185895 254 3)
Wignall, C. J. *Complete British Railways Maps & Gazetteer from 1830-1981*
    (OPC, 1983; ISBN 0 86093 162 5)

Acknowledgements

My thanks go to the Llangollen Railway, Gwili Railway, Barry Rail Centre, Telford Steam Railway and Arriva Trains Wales for their help with dates and other information, and to Richard Casserley, Philip Halling, Kevin Heywood, John McCrickard, Brian Mills, Geoff Richards, Dave Sallery, Paul Shannon, John Stretton and Dave Walters for the use of their photographs and/or news, helping me to keep up to date with changes. Thanks go to my wife, Geraldine, for all her help and support. Thanks particularly to Terry Gough, who instigated the series, for all his assistance, photographs and advice.

Introduction

This volume covers Wales, the Borders and Merseyside, and includes a wide range of stations from tiny platforms such as Cefn Tilla Halt to main-line stations such as Telford Central. It has to be said that most of the new stations are rather basic, such as those on the relatively recently reopened branch to Ebbw Vale. But they offer waiting shelters, often nearby parking facilities and, above all, a regular rail service. There are, however, some modern and impressive new stations, such as Liverpool South Parkway. Figures of passenger usage of these new stations have been very encouraging in most cases and have far exceeded expectations.

Looking into the future, with regard to the opening of new stations there are a number in the pipeline and under consideration. These include a new £6.5 million station in Ebbw Vale town centre, by extending the services on the Ebbw Vale branch and by offering Newport as an alternative destination to Cardiff. There is also the possibility of the branch from Pantyffynnon to Gwaun-cae-Gurwen being reopened to passenger services. The heritage lines, too, have a number of plans, of which the extension to Corwen on the Llangollen Railway is one of the most important; another involves the Gwili Railway, which would bring the railway nearer to Carmarthen. Following the opening of the extension to Blaenavon on the Pontypool & Blaenavon Railway in 2010, work is well advanced on the branch to Big Pit. The Telford Steam Railway now runs trains from Horsehay & Dawley, with extensions in progress. There seems a good chance that a service will run from Bangor to Llangefni on Anglesey, while looking further ahead there are plans at Oswestry and Garw, so there is a great deal to look forward to!

The photographs are all my own unless otherwise credited.

Using this book

The stations that qualify for inclusion are listed in geographical order, starting in south-west Wales and finishing on Merseyside. For each station the name (with, where applicable, the Welsh name) is accompanied by the map reference in Baker's *Rail Atlas of Great Britain & Ireland* (see the Bibliography) – the page number followed by the grid reference. Some stations are not marked in the atlas, in which case the reference is shown in brackets. Then follow the various opening and closing dates, and references, where appropriate, to any other photographs of the location that have been published in Past & Present Publishing's 'British Railways Past & Present' (P&P) and 'Past & Present Companion' (P&PC) series (again, see the Bibliography). Under 'Operator' are listed the owning company at the Grouping in 1923, and the current organisation managing the station (Train Operating Company or Network Rail), or the operator in the case of a heritage line (only standard-gauge lines are included). Where a station is no longer open, I have entered the name of the operator at closure. For reopened lines, the dates refer to use by passenger trains.

Please note that details of train services given in this book are correct at the time of publication, but will vary in the future. Always check with the operator before travelling. The criteria for inclusion of stations and lines in this book are given in the first volume of the series.

John Hillmer
Wilmslow

Fishguard & Goodwick (Abergwaun ac Wdig)

29, A2

Previous name	Goodwick	
Opened	1 July 1899	
Closed	6 April 1964; service for workmen's trains to Trecwn continued until 3 August 1964	
Reopened	19 June 1965	
Closed	16 September 1972	
Reopened	possibly 2012	
P&P	No 38, p63	
Operator original	GWR	
current	none	

The first reopening was for summer motorail services from Kensington Olympia, although the public timetable quoted Fishguard Harbour as the station. The motorail service continued to run until the early 1980s. From September 2011 the service to Fishguard Harbour was dramatically improved, which could lead to the reopening of the station.

The abandoned station on 16 May 2000 looking towards Harbour station. *Terry Gough*

Penally (Penalun) 30, B1

Opened		October 1863
Closed		15 June 1964
Reopened		29 June 1970
Closed		16 November 1970
Reopened		5 April 1971
Closed		13 September 1971
Reopened		28 February 1972
P&P		No 38, p33
Operator	**original**	GWR
	current	ATW

The rather bare platform is very long, lengthening having been completed by 14 March 1906, as the station was used by troops arriving for military exercises in South Pembrokeshire. In the period 2007/8 the annual passenger usage was just over 4,500. Trains run between Pembroke Dock and Carmarthen or on to Swansea, with a few extended to Cardiff Central. The service on Mondays to Saturdays is approximately 2-hourly, with limited services on Sundays.

Penally station looking first towards Tenby on 29 June 1994, then towards Manorbier on 17 May 2000. Author/ *Terry Gough*

Bronwydd Arms   30, A2

Opened	3 September 1860	The current station was opened by the Gwili Railway in 1978.
Closed	31 December 1860	
Reopened	12 August 1861	
Closed	22 February 1965	
Reopened	25 March 1978	
P&P	No 38, pp95-96	
Operator original	GWR	
current	GwilR	

8.1 Great Western Railway uw

BRONWYDD ARMS

ADMIT ONE to Platform 1d

This Ticket must be given up on leaving Platform & available one hour. For conditions See back p.m

Terry Gough collection

Above: The road crossing at Bronwydd Arms on 21 May 2000, showing the signal box, platform and semaphore signals. *Terry Gough*

Right: Bronwydd Arms looking in the opposite direction (towards Carmarthen), also on 21 May 2000, showing the main station building with the level crossing gates beyond. *Terry Gough*

Llwyfan Cerrig   30, A2

Opened		17 April 1987
Operator	original	GwilR
	current	GwilR

The station was built by the Gwili Railway and was the terminus for trains from Bronwydd Arms until the extension to Danycoed was built. There is no road access to the station and passengers alighting here must continue their journey by train. A picnic area is provided. The station building came from Felin Fach.

Left: A busy few moments on the platform at Llwyfan Cerrig on 25 June 1993 as No 71516 *Welsh Guardsman* prepares for departure. *John Stretton*

Below: Danycoed station on 3 June 2010. *Geoff Richards*

Danycoed   30, A2

Opened	1 March 2001
Operator original	GwilR
current	GwilR

This was also built by the present owners and is the current northern terminus of the line. There is no road access and passengers have to return to Bronwydd Arms by train.

Conwil   30, A2

Opened		3 September 1860
Closed		31 December 1860
Reopened		15 August 1861
Closed		22 February 1965
Reopened		no date proposed
Operator	original	GWR
	current	none

The next station on the Gwili Railway's route is Conwil (Cynwyl Elfed). It lies adjacent to a main road, but it is likely to be many years before the line is extended beyond Danycoed.

Left: Conwil station on 21 May 2000.
Terry Gough

Below: The site acquired by the Gwili Railway for its Carmarthen station, photographed on 9 October 2009.
Geoff Richards

Carmarthen North   30, A2

Opened	not yet opened
Operator (future)	GwiR

The Gwili Railway intends to extend south in the near future, and a site for its station on the outskirts of Carmarthen has been acquired.

Sugar Loaf   31,A1

Opened	1899 as staff halt; from 10 June 1909 for schoolchildren and market use on Fridays (not in public timetable); ceased 1965; 1984 for ramblers, up trains only; 1985, for one Saturday train per month; 1987 and 1989, on summer Sundays and Bank Holidays, on request; 17 May 1992, first appearance in public timetable; 28 May 1995, daily all-year service introduced	The station is very isolated, located between Cynghordy and Llanwrtyd in Powys. It is 820 feet above sea level and is a request stop. Currently there are four services a day Monday to Saturday, reduced to two on Sundays. It is reputed to have been the 14th least-used station in the UK in the 2002/3 financial year, with only 99 fare-paying passengers, and it was not very different in 2007/8 with 111. The trains run from Swansea to Shrewsbury via Llanelli, with one service starting from Cardiff Central. It is known as the 'Heart of Wales Line', and is supported by a Community Rail Partnership and a Travellers Association.
P&PC	*The Central Wales Line*, pp45-46	
Operator original	LNWR	
current	ATW	

This 20 May 1995 photograph shows the total isolation of the station with its very short platform.

Swansea Direct Line (Lonlas Junction-Felin Fran)

31, A2

Opened	18 February 1912
Closed	no date available for cessation of passenger trains; remained open for freight
Reopened	21 June 2002 for passenger trains
P&P	No 37, p90
Operator original	GWR
current	NR

The Swansea District Line ran from Skewen East Junction and Jersey Marine South/Lonlas Junction to Felin Fran, opened in 1912, and from Felin Fran to Morlais Junction (where it meets the Heart of Wales Line) on 14 July 1913, to enable trains to bypass Swansea. It was (and still is) used mainly by freight, as there is little point in passenger trains omitting Swansea. The one exception is the Paddington/Cardiff-Fishguard Harbour trains, which started using this route again after many years in 2002. Proposals were made in 2005 to reinstate the line for an hourly service between Cardiff and West Wales, with new parkway-style stations at Llandarcy, Morriston and Grovesend, but as yet with no result.

A Fishguard-Cardiff train hauled by Class 37 No 37418 is seen near Lonlas Tunnel, one of the line's three tunnels, on 18 July 2002. Felin Fran is some distance beyond the rear of the train. *Terry Gough*

Swansea Direct Line   32, A1
(Jersey Marine North-Dynevor Junction)

Opened	9 May 1915	The section between Jersey Marine North and Dynevor Junction opened in 1915, enabling trains to get to the Swansea District Line from Court Sart Junction (on the main line at Briton Ferry) instead of continuing on the main line to Skewen.
Closed	no date available for cessation of passenger trains; remained open for freight trains and occasional excursion trains	
Reopened	21 June 2002 for passenger trains	
Operator original	GWR	
current	NR	

Right: On 3 September 2003 Class 37 No 37422 heads a passenger train from Fishguard to Cardiff on the left, about to cross with Class 66 No 66236, hauling a down train of coal hoppers. *Terry Gough*

Flying Loop Junction (Briton Ferry)   32, A1

Opened	1935	Trains from the Swansea District Line join the main line at this junction, which is close to Court Sart Junction used by trains to the District Line.
Closed	no date available for cessation of passenger trains; remained open for freight trains	
Reopened	21 June 2002 for passenger trains	
P&P	No 37, p23	
Operator original	GWR	
current	NR	

Right: On 18 July 2002 No 60046 approaches Flying Loop Junction at the end of the Swansea District Line with a coal train from Swansea Burrows to Aberthaw Power Station. The only passenger train of the day was not due for several hours. The main line is visible on the left. *Terry Gough*

Llansamlet   31, A2

Previous name	Llansamlet North
Opened	1 April 1852
Closed	1 January 1885
Reopened	1 January 1885 on new site
Closed	2 November 1964
Reopened	27 June 1994 between the earlier sites
Operator original	GWR
current	ATW

The main line between Swansea and Cardiff is known as the 'Swanline'. On Monday to Saturday the service is approximately hourly or 2-hourly, with no Sunday service. Westbound services originate primarily at Cardiff Central, with some at Manchester Piccadilly with destinations of Swansea, Carmarthen, Milford Haven or Pembroke Dock. Eastbound trains are primarily to Cardiff Central.

Left: The up platform looking west on 9 May 1995.

Below: The platforms are staggered – looking east towards Skewen the down platform can be seen beyond the road bridge.

A four-coach local train, led by unit No 150279, calls at the station en route to Milford Haven on 18 July 2002. *Terry Gough*

Virgin Cross Country trains pass through Llansamlet, in this instance the 15.24 Swansea High Street to Birmingham New Street service, also on 18 July 2002. The leading power car is No 43166 and on the rear is No 43089. *Terry Gough*

Skewen (Sgiwen)   32, A1

Previous name		Dynevor
Opened		June 1882
Closed		1 May 1910
Reopened		1 May 1910 on new site
Closed		2 November 1964
Reopened		27 June 1994 on another new site
Operator	original	GWR
	current	ATW

The station lies between Llansamlet and Neath, and in the period 2007/8 the annual rail passenger usage was just over 17,000. In the summer timetable of 2011, on Mondays to Saturdays there was an hourly or 2-hourly service, with no trains on Sundays.

Above: Class 158 No 158838 heads west on 18 July 2002. *Terry Gough*

Below: Looking in the opposite direction on 9 May 1995 the line runs straight towards the site of Skewen East Junction.

Briton Ferry (Llansawel)   32, A1

Previous names	Briton Ferry West, Briton Ferry East
Opened	2 September 1850; 'West' added 1 July 1924
Closed	8 July 1935
Opened	14 March 1895; 'East' added 1 July 1924
Closed	16 September 1935
Reopened	16 September 1935, on new site
Closed	2 November 1964
Reopened	1 June 1994, on another new site
P&P	No 37, pp24-27
Operator original	CR/GWR (Briton Ferry West); RSBR/ GWR (Briton Ferry East)
current	ATW

There have been three other stations with the same name, from the first in 1850 to the final one, which closed in 1964. Following closure of the two original stations in 1935, services were diverted to a new station, then when that closed there was no station serving Briton Ferry until the present station was opened 30 years later. In the 2007/8 period the annual passenger usage was more than 22,500. Currently on Mondays to Saturdays there is an hourly or 2-hourly service, with no trains on Sundays.

Left: Looking west on 9 May 1995, No 143610 calls with a service from Swansea to Cardiff Central.

Below left: Class 37 No 37418 heads a Cardiff to Fishguard service on 18 July 2002. On this occasion the train made an unscheduled stop to let a passenger alight, as she was on the wrong train. The platforms are partly staggered, and each is 120 yards long. *Terry Gough*

Below: The holding sidings, seen on the right on 9 May 1995, are used for coal and other block trains.

Baglan   32, B1

Opened	2 June 1996	The station was a latecomer to Swanline. It is located west of Port Talbot and was built at a cost of £650,000 with twin 106-yard-long platforms and shelters. Currently on Mondays to Saturdays there is an hourly or 2-hourly service, with no trains on Sundays.
Operator original	RR	
current	ATW	

Left: Baglan's modern station looking west on 5 June 1996.

Class 37s Nos 37896 and 37701 work an up loaded coal train on the same day; both locomotives are in Transrail livery.

Pyle (Y Pîl) — 31, A1

Opened	19 June 1850	The first station was relocated and amalgamated with the former Llynvi & Ogmore Railway station in 1876. It closed under the Beeching cuts. The current station, between Port Talbot Parkway and Bridgend, was opened about half a mile to the west, and was built with financial assistance from Mid and West Glamorgan County Councils. The annual passenger usage over the last four years has varied between 43,000 and 48,000. Currently on Mondays to Saturdays there is an hourly or 2-hourly service, with no trains on Sundays. Trains stop at all stations from Bridgend to Swansea, while some head further west to Pembroke Dock or Milford Haven.
Re-sited	13 November 1876	
Closed	2 November 1964	
Reopened	27 June 1994 (resited)	
P&P	No 28, p146	
Operator original	SWR/GWR	
current	ATW	

Left: Class 47 No 47714 (in Res livery) heads 1A71, the Swansea to Paddington mail train, on 9 May 1995.

Below: Looking west, the down platform can be seen on the left beyond the footbridge, with the up platform opposite.

Maesteg   p31, C1

Previous name	Castle Street
Opened	1 July 1924 (Castle Street)
Closed	22 June 1970
Reopened	28 September 1992 (resited)
P&P	No 28, p151 (Castle Street)
Operator original	GWR
current	ATW

£3.3 million was spent to provide six new stations and three Class 143 diesel trains for the Maesteg branch. Built on former sidings, the new Maesteg station opened with investment from Mid Glamorgan County Council and the EEC. The new platform was relocated some 200 yards down the line and closer to the town centre than the original Castle Street station. In the period 2007/08 the annual rail passenger use was just short of 160,000. Currently on Mondays to Saturdays there is an hourly service, with no trains on Sundays. Under consideration is an extension of the line to the north.

Above: This photograph was taken from the town side on 28 June 1995 and shows the car park, station entrance and shelter.

Right: Class 143 No 143610 has just arrived on the same day and will return shortly to Cardiff Central.

Beyond Maesteg station is the freight line, now out of use, which led to the St John Washery, north of the town. Seen from the abandoned line on 19 September 2001 is No 143609 in the station. *Terry Gough*

Maesteg (Ewenny Road) (Maesteg Heol Ewenny)

31, C1

Opened	26 October 1992
Operator original	RR
current	ATW

This new station, with capital investment by Mid Glamorgan County Council, was built to serve local housing and industry. The annual passenger usage figure for 2007/8 was just over 4,500. The service is every hour from Monday to Saturday, with no Sunday service. Trains from the branch normally terminate at Cardiff Central or Gloucester.

These views are looking north on 28 June 1995.

Garth   p31, C1

Previous name	Troedyrhiw Garth
Opened	1873 (first time in Bradshaw)
Closed	22 June 1970 to public, 14 July for schoolchildren
Reopened	28 September 1992 (resited)
Operator original	GWR
current	ATW

South of the current location there was an earlier station known as Troedyrhiw Garth, which closed in 1970. There was also a station named Garth on the line from Port Talbot, but this had closed in 1913 and was replaced by a station named Cwmdu, which itself closed in 1932. When the new Garth station opened in 1992 there was considerable local debate whether to call the station by the old name, because of the potential confusion with another Garth station, located on the Heart of Wales Line. It was built with investment from Mid Glamorgan County Council, and passenger numbers were nearly 18,000 for 2007/8. Currently the train service on Mondays to Saturdays is hourly, with no Sunday service. All services call at the five intermediate stations on the branch.

Class 158 No 158834 is about to leave Garth northwards for Maesteg on 28 June 1995.

Tondu   31, C2

Previous name	Tondu Junction
Opened	25 February 1864
Closed	22 June 1970
Reopened	28 September 1992
P&P	No 28, pp152-153
Operator original	GWR
current	ATW

Tondu is the junction with the freight-only line from Margam to Blaengarw, which leaves the Maesteg line north of the station to the east, beyond the signal box. The box is of GWR design, dating back to 1884, formerly named Tondu Middle. There is just a single platform, with services from Cardiff Central to Maesteg, many starting at Gloucester, providing an hourly service. There are currently no Sunday trains. The annual rail passenger service has remained consistent over the last four years, around 28,000 to nearly 31,000 in 2006/7, then dropping back to just short of 28,500 in 2007/8.

The car park is seen on 28 June 1995, with semaphore junction signals and the signal box beyond the footbridge.

Above: A closer view of the semaphore signals and Tondu signal box taken from the northern end of the platform on 28 June 1995

Below: Looking south from the footbridge, on the same day.

Sarn		31,C2
Opened	**28 September 1992**	This new station was opened with capital investment from Mid Glamorgan County Council. The annual passenger usage has increased from just over 27,000 in 2004/5 to nearly 34,000 in 2007/8. On Mondays to Saturdays there is an hourly service, but no Sunday operation. Many of the trains from Maesteg go to Gloucester.
Operator original	RR	
current	ATW	

Sarn station looking towards Tondu, with Class 143 No 143610 forming a service to Maesteg on 28 June 1995.

Wildmill (Melin Wyllt) — 31, C2

Opened:	16 November 1992; closed same day for safety reasons.	Built with capital assistance from Mid Glamorgan County Council, the station's annual rail passenger rate has been fairly consistent between just over 10,000 in 2004/5 to 12,500 in 2007/8. The service is hourly on Mondays to Saturdays, with no Sunday service. Most services operate from Maesteg to Gloucester.
Reopened	12 December 1992	
Operator original	RR	
current	ATW	

The single platform looking south towards Bridgend on 28 June 1995.

Llantwit Major (Llanilltud Fawr)   7, A2

Opened	1 December 1897	The service on the Vale of Glamorgan line is currently hourly Mondays to Saturdays, with a Sunday service that varies with the time of year, in winter approximately every 2 hours. In the three years to 2007-2008 the annual rail passenger usage has risen from 209,000 to 260,000.
Closed	15 June 1964	
Reopened	12 June 2005	
P&P	No 28, p119	
Operator original	Barry Railway	
current	ATW	

Left: Class 142 unit No 142075 heads west towards Bridgend 15 May 2007.

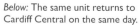

Below: The same unit returns to Cardiff Central on the same day.

Rhoose Cardiff International Airport   7, A2
(Y Rhws Maes Awyr Rhyngwladol Caerdydd)

Previous name	Rhoose	The station was reopened primarily to cater for travellers using Cardiff Airport, and a regular bus service connects the station and the airport. The annual rail passenger usage has risen from 101,000 in 2005/6 to just short of 166,000 in 2007/8. The service is currently hourly Mondays to Saturdays, with a Sunday service that varies with the time of year, in winter approximately every 2 hours. Trains run between Merthyr Tydfil and Bridgend.
Opened	1 December 1897	
Closed 15 June 1964		
Reopened	12 June 2005	
P&P	No 28, p117	
Operator original	Barry Railway	
current	ATW	

The first view, looking west on 15 May 2007, is from the end of the Cardiff platform. The platforms are staggered on either side of the crossing, as can be seen clearly in the second photograph.

Eastbrook   27, C2

Opened	24 November 1986
Operator original	BR
current	ATW

The station was built at a cost of £160,000, funded jointly by South Glamorgan County Council and grants from ERDF and PRNI in cooperation with Regional Railways. It has twin platforms with shelters and footbridge, together with car parking. The most recent annual rail usage was more than 160,000. On Mondays to Saturdays there is a frequent service of four trains an hour in each direction, with approximately three an hour on Sundays, additionally from Treherbert and Rhymney. Most services run from Abercynon, Aberdare or Merthyr Tydfil to Barry Island.

Eastbrook station on 21 September 1994.

Barry Island/Plymouth Road (Ynys y Barri)   27, C1

Opened	3 August 1896
Opened (Plymouth Road platform)	1 June 1997; first train April 1998
Closed	28 December 2008 (Vale of Glamorgan preserved part only)
Reopened	September 2009 (Barry Tourist Railway)
P&P	No 28, pp112-113
Operator original	GWR
current	BRC and ATW

At one time the line continued to the original terminus at Barry Pier, but the tunnel leading to this station has been blocked off and is used as a shooting range. The Pier station opened on 27 June 1899 and connected with steamer services. The last train for steamers ran on 11 October 1971, although occasional steamers called in 1972 and 1973, but with no rail connection. ATW uses the Barry end of one platform for its services, leaving the rest of the station and associated lines to be developed as a heritage centre. The first preservation scheme foundered, resulting in closure, but the railway reopened under a new operator (Cambrian Transport) nine months later. It is hoped to run regular passenger trains over 2 miles of line in the near future. ATW services comprise three per hour on Monday to Saturday, with a total of two per hour on Sundays from Treherbert, Aberdare, Rhymney or Cardiff.

The main station building at Barry, seen here on 11 September 2007, dates back to 1896.

The view from Barry Island station looking towards the Pier (out of sight) on 10 March 1998. To the left is Plymouth Road station, museum and engine shed.

A more recent photograph dated 11 September 2007 shows the truncated line used by ATW and loss of track to the other platform. The heritage line toward Barry is to the left of the iron railings.

Waterfront (Hood Road)			27, C1
Opened		13 September 2002	This is the terminus of a short spur from the heritage line towards Barry, and is next to a retail park of the same name.
Operator	**original**	VGR	
	current	BRC	

Waterfront (Hood Road) station in June 2010. *Brian Mills*

Woodham Halt   (27, C1)

Opened		8 April 2004
Operator	original	VGR
	current	BRC

The halt is situated just beyond Barry (ATW station) and has public access.

Woodham Halt in June 2010.
Brian Mills

Gladstone Bridge Platform   (27, C1)

Opened		March 2008
Operator	original	VGR
	current	BRC

This station also has public access and is situated parallel to the main Network Rail line. It is planned to extend the heritage line to terminate at a new station adjacent to Barry Docks station, which is served by ATW.

Gladstone Bridge Platform in June 2010. *Brian Mills*

Pencoed   31, C2

Opened	2 September 1850	
Closed	2 November 1964	
Reopened	11 May 1992	
Operator	**original**	GWR
	current	ATW

This station, between Bridgend and Llanharan, was built with the financial assistance of Mid Glamorgan County Council, with platforms that are staggered on either side of the level crossing. The signal box (Pencoed Crossing) was taken out of use at the end of March 2007 and demolished the following week. The annual passenger usage has risen from nearly 165,000 in 2004/5 to almost 194,000 in 2007/8. Currently on Mondays to Saturdays there is an hourly service, but no trains on Sundays.

Right: An unidentified Class 60 heads east through the station on 28 June 1995.

Below: An HST approaches the down platform with a Swansea-bound service on the same day.

Llanharan 31, C2

		There was an earlier station on this site, between Pencoed and Pontyclun, which closed in the Beeching era. There are two platforms, with modest waiting shelters, connected by a footbridge. Because trains were running when the new station was built, a type of construction called Corus Modular Platform was used. In the first year of operation the rail passenger usage was more than 27,000. Currently on Mondays to Saturdays there is an hourly service, but no trains on Sundays. Most services (originating at Maesteg) terminate either at Cardiff Central or Gloucester.
Opened	1 September 1899	
Closed	2 November 1964	
Reopened	10 December 2007	
Operator original	GWR	
current	ATW	

Left: This 16 July 2009 photograph was taken from the station footbridge looking towards Pencoed.

Below: A platform-level view looking towards Pontyclun.

Pontyclun   31, C2

Previous name	Llantrisant	The new station was opened with financial assistance from Mid Glamorgan County Council. The annual passenger use in 2007/8 was well over 200,000. Currently on Mondays to Saturdays there is an hourly service, but no trains on Sundays
Opened	19 June 1850 (as Llantrissant, later Llantrisant)	
Closed	2 November 1964	
Reopened	28 September 1992 (resited)	
P&P	No 28, p137 (Llantrisant)	
Operator original	GWR	
current	ATW	

Above: Looking west on 3 August 1995, unit No 143619 leaves for Maesteg.

Right: Looking from the station footbridge in the same direction on the same day, the entrance to Llantrisant Yard is on the right, at that time operated by Transrail. The yard gave access to Cwm coking plant.

Ninian Park (Parc Ninian) 27, B2

Previous names	Ninian Park Platform, Ninian Park Halt
Opened	2 November 1912, for intermittent football use (Cardiff City); June 1934, for normal Sunday services
Closed	3 September 1939, for normal services
Closed	1977, last regular use for football having been during 1966/67 season.
Reopened	5 October 1987, for regular public use
Operator original	GWR
current	ATW

Ninian Park is one of four stations on this 5-mile route known as the 'City Line'. Following the rather chequered history of Cardiff City Football Club, the current modernised station was opened with financial assistance from South Glamorgan County Council and grants from ERDF and PRNI, and serves the Leckwith and South Canton areas of Cardiff. Because of the connection with football, being situated near the former Cardiff City stadium, the platforms are the longest on the line, taking up to nine coaches. The latest published figures of annual passenger usage are more than 35,000. Currently the service is every half-hour on Monday-Saturday, running between Cardiff Central and Radyr; there is no Sunday service.

Above: No 150271 calls at Ninian Park with a service to Coryton on 12 April 1995.

Right: Looking north towards Radyr on the same day, the Leckwith loop, which connects with the South Wales main line, can be seen diverging to the right.

Waun-Gron Park (Parc Waun-gron)		27, B1
Opened	2 November 1987	The station serves the Fairwater area of Cardiff. On Monday to Saturday there is currently a service every half-hour between Cardiff Central and Radyr, but no Sunday service. When opened, the station was experimental, funded by South Glamorgan County Council at a cost of £180,000. In the 2007/8 period the annual passenger usage was more than 25,000. The platforms are slightly staggered.
Operator original	BR	
current	ATW	

The first photograph is looking north towards Fairwater on 12 April 1995, and the second in the opposite direction, on 28 February 1996.

Fairwater (Y Tyllgoed)   27, B1

Opened	5 October 1987	The station was opened with investment from South
Operator original	BR	Glamorgan County Council and grants from ERDF and
current	ATW	PRNI working with Regional Railways. During the last four years, the annual passenger usage has risen from 18,000-plus to well over 25,000. The Monday to Saturday service is half-hourly, but there are no Sunday trains.

Right: A distant view looking north towards Danescourt on 12 April 1995, showing the rural surroundings.

Below: A close-up of the station, looking in the same direction.

Danescourt   27, A1

Opened		5 October 1987
Operator	original	BR
	current	ATW

A comparison with Fairwater shows the similarity of design. Investment assistance came from South Glamorgan County Council, together with grants from ERDF and PRNI in cooperation with British Rail. Annual rail passenger usage in the 2007/8 period was nearly 65,000. Mondays to Saturdays there is normally a half-hourly service between Cardiff Central and Radyr, but no Sunday service.

No 150271 has just left the station en route to Cardiff Central on 12 April 1995.

Looking north towards Radyr on the same day.

Cathays
27, B2

Previous name	Woodville Road Halt
Opened	July 1906
Closed	15 September 1958
Reopened	3 October 1983 (resited)
P&P	No 28, pp52 & 53
Operator original	GWR
current	ATW

This was the first new station to be opened in South Wales for more than 40 years, located between Cardiff Queen Street and Radyr to serve the University and business area to the north of the city, and just south of the original station. The joint funding from South Glamorgan County Council in cooperation with Regional Railways amounted to more than £80,000. The twin platforms are of pre-cast concrete. Initially a target of 600 passenger journeys per day was anticipated, and this was reached within the first three months. Traffic has risen by more than 20% since then, and in 2007/8 amounted to half a million passenger journeys. There are up to six trains an hour on Monday to Saturday, and between one and three per hour on Sundays. The majority of trains run from Barry Island to Merthyr Tydfil or to Aberdare.

Looking north-west towards Llandaf and Radyr on 2 September 1994.

Ystrad Rhondda 31, C2

		The original Ystrad Rhondda station (opened in 1861), on the Treherbert branch between Llwynypia and Ton Pentre, has been renamed Ton Pentre, and never closed. The new Ystrad Rhondda serves Ystrad in Rhondda Cynon Taf. Built with capital investment from Mid Glamorgan County Council, there are two platforms each 100 yards long and the station is a passing place. By 2007/8 the annual usage was more than 72,000. Monday to Saturdays there are basically two trains an hour in each direction, and on Sundays every 2 hours. Most services operate between Cardiff Central and Treherbert.
Opened	29 September 1986	
Operator original	TVR	
current	ATW	

Right and below: Looking north on 26 April 1995 – note the long footbridge.

Ynyswen   31, B2

Previous name	Tylacoch	This station, between Treorchy and Treherbert, was built with capital investment from Mid Glamorgan County Council, and serves the village of Ynyswen in Rhondda Cynon Taf. It achieved a more than threefold increase in forecasted traffic in the early years, and annual passenger usage has remained fairly static in the last few years; during 2007/8 it was just over 8,500. Currently, on Monday-Saturday there are basically two trains an hour in each direction, and on Sundays every 2 hours. Services operate primarily between Treherbert and Cardiff Central.
Opened	October 1906	
Closed	1912 (last appearance in Bradshaw)	
Reopened	29 September 1986 (possibly on new site)	
Operator original	TVR	
current	ATW	

Class 150 No 150278 operates a service to Barry Island on 26 April 1995. Both views are looking north.

Abercynon North (Abercynon Gogledd) 31, C2

Opened	3 October 1988	On the Aberdare branch between Pontypridd and Penrhiwceiber, this station was opened with capital investment from Mid Glamorgan County Council. It was very close to Abercynon South, and in November 2007 a proposal was submitted by the Welsh Assembly to cease all services provided by the North station, and to transfer them to South.
Closed	end May 2008	
Operator original	BR	
at closure	ATW	

Class 150 No 150266 is seen departing north to Aberdare on 2 September 1994.

Penrhiwceiber   31, B2

Previous name	Penrhiwceiber Low Level (in 1924)	Located between Pontypridd and Mountain Ash, the station closed in 1964 but was refurbished and reopened in 1988 with capital investment from Mid Glamorgan County Council. In the period 2007/8 the annual passenger usage was nearly 70,000. On Mondays to Saturdays there are two services per hour, and every 2 hours on Sundays. Trains run mostly from Aberdare to Barry Island.
Opened	1 June 1883	
Closed	16 March 1964	
Reopened	3 October 1988	
Operator original	TVR	
current	ATW	

Above: No 143609 arrives en route to Barry Island on 8 June 1995.

Left: The simple basic platform, looking south.

Mountain Ash (Aberpennar) 31, B2

Previous name	Oxford Street	
Opened	6 August 1846	
Closed	16 March 1964	
Reopened	3 October 1988 (resited) 29 January 2001 (resited again on deviation to east)	
Operator original	TVR	
current	ATW	

Opened with capital investment from Mid Glamorgan County Council, the annual rail passenger usage in the financial period 2007/8 was more than 115,000. Most services run from Aberdare to Barry Island; on Mondays to Saturdays there are two services per hour, and every 2 hours on Sundays.

Left: The basic single platform of the 1988 station looking north on 8 June 1995.

Below: Class 143 No 143609 is seen leaving for Aberdare.

The current Mountain Ash (New) station, looking north on 16 July 2008, note now with double track.

Fernhill		31, B2
Opened	3 October 1988	Opened with investment by Mid-Glamorgan County Council, the annual rail passenger usage in the 2007/8 period was more than 26,000. On Mondays to Saturdays there are two services per hour, and every 2 hours on Sundays.
Operator original	BR	
current	ATW	

Fernhill station looking north on 8 June 1995.

Cwmbach   31, B2

Previous name	Cwmbach Halt	Located between Fernhill and Aberdare, during 2005 the length of the single platform was doubled to allow four-car units to stop at the station. Annual passenger numbers were around 20,000 in 2007/8. On Mondays to Saturdays there are two services per hour, and every 2 hours on Sundays.
Opened	12 July 1914	
Closed	15 June 1964	
Reopened	3 October 1988	
Operator original	GWR	
current	ATW	

Looking north on 8 June 1995, Class 143 No 143616 leaves for Aberdare.

Aberdare (Aberdâr)   31, B2

Previous name	Aberdare High Level
Opened	24 September 1851
Closed	15 June 1964
Reopened	3 October 1988 (resited)
P&P	No 26, pp92-93 (HL)
Operator original	GWR
current	ATW

The new station was opened with joint investment capital from Mid-Glamorgan County Council and the EEC, and was one of six two-car platforms built on the branch at a cost of £450,000. The platform has undergone work to lengthen it to accomodate four-car units. Annual rail passenger usage in the 2007/8 period was approaching half a million. On Mondays to Saturdays there are two services per hour, and every 2 hours on Sundays. Mostly trains run to Barry Island.

Left: Looking north on 8 June 1995, showing the old High Level station on the right-hand side beyond the new station.

Below: Class 143 No 143611 forms a service to Barry Island on the same day.

Lisvane & Thornhill (Llysfaen a Draenan Pen-y-Graig)   2, A2

Previous names	Cefn On Halt, Cefn-Onn	This station, on the Rhymney Valley branch between Caerphilly and Llanishen, cost £181,000 with investment from British Rail and South Glamorgan County Council. It replaced the hardly used Cefn-Onn station, which had only footpath access and was a short distance to the north. Cefn-Onn remained open for several months after the opening of the replacement station. Annual rail passenger usage increased to more than 150,000 in the 2007/8 financial period, and there is currently a service on Monday to Saturday every 15 minutes, starting at Rhymney or Bargoed and travelling towards Penarth, and on Sundays one every 2 hours between Barry Island and Rhymney.
Opened	October 1915 (first appearance in Bradshaw)	
Closed	29 September 1986	
Reopened	4 November 1985 (resited)	
P&P	No 28, p24	
Operator original	Rhymney Railway	
current	ATW	

Above: Class 143 No 143602 heads for Caerphilly on 6 October 1994.

Right: Class 150 No 150267 arrives from the north en route to Penarth on the same day.

Ticket - *Terry Gough collection*

Ty Glas (Y Ty Glas) 27, A2

Opened		29 April 1987
Operator	original	BR
	current	ATW

This is the first station on the Coryton branch from Heath Low Level, and opened with financial support from South Glamorgan County Council, ERDF and PRNI. Until 11 May 1987 it was a request stop only. The platform will hold a two-car unit and was opened experimentally to serve housing, business and industrial areas nearby, at a cost of £78,000. Annual usage increased to more than 60,000 passengers in the 2007/8 period. It has a mainly half-hourly service on Monday to Saturday, but no Sunday service. Trains normally go to Cardiff Central, having started at Coryton.

Looking west towards Birchgrove on 6 October 1994.

Rogerstone (Y Tŷ Du)   32, C1

Previous names	Tydee, Tydu
Opened	1851 (first appearance in Bradshaw)
Closed	30 April 1962
Reopened	6 February 2008
Operator original	GWR
current	ATW

This is the first station on the Ebbw Vale branch between Cardiff Central and Risca, and was a replacement for the original station, which was half a mile south. It is situated on the site of former rail sidings serving Rogerstone Power Station, which became a redevelopment area for housing. It has a single platform with a covered waiting area, accessed by steps and a ramp from the car park. Although much nearer to Newport, all trains run from Cardiff Central, a distance of 14 miles, but future plans include an hourly service to Newport. In the 2007/8 period the annual passenger usage was 10,760. The current service is hourly Monday to Saturday, and every 2 hours on Sundays.

Above: A northbound train is about to continue its journey on 19 August 2009.

Right: The modern car parking area, and the waiting shelter on the platform.

Risca & Pontymister (Rhisga a Phont-y-meistr) 32, C1

Previous name	Risca	Located approximately half a mile south of the original Risca station, between Rogerstone and Cross Keys, the site was originally railway sidings. There are twin platforms, and in the first year of opening more than 21,000 passengers used the station. Currently, there is an hourly service from Monday to Saturday, and every 2 hours on Sundays. All trains originate at Cardiff Central, although there are plans for an additional service from Newport.
Opened	23 December 1850	
Closed	30 April 1962	
Reopened	6 February 2008 (resited)	
Operator original	GWR	
current	ATW	

An unidentified Class 150 unit is about to leave for Ebbw Vale Parkway on 19 August 2009.

Above: The two platforms at Risca & Pontymister are backed by new housing on the right.

Below: Unit No 150242 leaves for Rogerstone and Cardiff Central, also on 19 August 2009.

Crosskeys   32, C1

Previous name	Cross Keys
Opened	September 1851
Closed	30 April 1962
Reopened	7 June 2008
Operator original	GWR
current	ATW

Built on the site of the former station, due to the compact nature of its position there is no dedicated station car park, but there is a public car park close by. The new station had the reputation of being one of the least busy in the UK however it has seen annual growth. Trains run every hour Monday to Saturday and every 2 hours on Sundays between Cardiff Central and Ebbw Vale. In the future an additional service on the branch is planned to run to and from Newport.

The first photograph, taken from the Cardiff platform on 19 August 2009, shows unit No 150242 arriving from Newbridge. Both views are looking north.

Newbridge (Trecelyn)   32, C1

Opened	23 December 1850	The station serves the towns of Newbridge and Blackwood and consists of a single platform built on the site of the former station and coal yard. In February 2009 Caerphilly County Borough Council started work on the construction of a footbridge to link the station with the Comprehensive School, Leisure Centre and town centre. In the first year of operation the station was used by more than 20,000 passengers, but in 2008/9 the figure had risen to in excess of 116,000. On Monday to Saturday there is currently an hourly service, and every 2 hours on Sundays.
Closed	30 April 1962	
Reopened	6 February 2008	
Operator original	GWR	
current	ATW	

Above: On 19 August 2009 unit No 150259 departs with a Cardiff Central service, passing under the long footbridge.

Left: Another unit of the same class pauses on the way to Ebbw Vale Parkway.

Llanhilleth (Llanhiledd)   32, B1

Opened	1 October 1901	The station was built near the site of the former station, and facilities include a car park. There is an hourly service on Mondays to Saturdays, reduced to every 2 hours on Sundays. Future plans include an additional hourly service on the branch to and from Newport, when a second platform will be built.
Closed	30 April 1962	
Reopened	27 April 2008	
Operator original	GWR	
current	ATW	

Class 150 No 150229 departs north for Ebbw Vale Parkway on 3 December 2009.
A new housing estate can be seen on the right.

Ebbw Vale Parkway (Parcffordd Glyn Ebwy)   32, B1

Previous name	Victoria
Opened	19 April 1852
Closed	30 April 1962
Reopened	6 February 2008 (resited)
Operator original	GWR
current	ATW

The new station is close to the site of the former Victoria station, and when it was opened the line had been freight-only for 46 years. In the first year of operation it was used by more than 50,000 passengers, but this increased markedly and the millionth passenger was recorded less than two years after opening. There is an hourly service on Monday-Saturday in each direction and every 2 hours on Sundays. There are plans to add a service to Newport, and in 2008 the Welsh Assembly announced a £2.6 million investment for improvements at Gaer Junction as an essential prerequisite to any future regular passenger service between Ebbw Vale and Newport.

Right: Looking south, unit No 150259 stands ready to leave for Cardiff Central on 16 July 2008.

Below: On the same day unit No 150258 has just arrived from Cardiff Central, to where it will return.

Blaenavon High Level   32, B1

Previous name	Blaenavon	Part of the Pontypool-Blaenavon-Brynmawr branch has been opened as a heritage line, the Pontypool & Blaenavon Railway. Blaenavon High Level station has been rebuilt and is on the edge of Blaenavon town.
Opened	18 December 1869	
Closed	5 May 1941	
Reopened	May 2010	
Operator original	LNWR	
current	PBR	

The approach to Blaenavon High Level on 21 August 2010. This is the southern terminus of the new line. *Terry Gough*

Above: Ex-BR Class 08 No 4157 (08927) enters the station on a train from Whistle Inn Halt. *Terry Gough* (Ticket *Terry Gough*)

Below: The end of the line on 5 June 2010 – although there are plans to extend further south to Varteg and eventually to the outskirts of Pontypool.

Furnace Sidings   32, B1

Opened	1983	Originally built to serve the mines, the railway was operated by the LNWR, taking coal to the industrial Midlands, although there was no station here. It later became a joint operation between the LNWR and GWR. The line closed to passengers in 1941 and to goods in 1954, although the Blaenavon to Pontypool section was in use for the nearby Big Pit and other local mines until 1980. Today Furnace Sidings is the headquarters of the railway, with associated sidings for storage of stock and workshops for maintenance and restoration. The Blaenavon area is a World Heritage Site, which includes the Big Pit National Coal Museum and Blaenavon Ironworks. A spur to Big Pit with a halt to serve the museum is opened on 16 Septemberg 2011.
Operator original	PBR	
current	PBR	

Left: A train from Blaenavon High Level approaches the station in appalling weather on 21 August 2010! To the left is the entrance to the sidings. The Big Pit branch leaves from the other side of the line beyond the station. *Terry Gough*

Below: The same formation leaves for Whistle Inn Halt, with the 08 on the rear. *Terry Gough*

Above: The footbridge is in the process of restoration; it was acquired from Hinckley and is of LNWR origin. *Terry Gough*

Below: No 71515 takes water at the northern end of Furnace Sidings station. This locomotive was built in 1944 and used by Mech Navvies Ltd in Northumberland until the 1970s. It was later used on the East Somerset Railway, then the Embsay & Bolton Abbey Steam Railway prior to recent transfer to its present location. *Terry Gough*

Whistle Inn Halt   32, B1

Previous names	Garn-yr-Erw Halt (original station), Whistle Inn (current station), Whistle Halt	The original station was north of the present site, immediately beyond the road bridge. It never appeared in the public timetable and was provided exclusively for miners. At 1,307 feet above sea level, it is the highest standard gauge station in England and Wales. There are ambitious proposals to extend the railway northward to Waunavon and Brynmawr, but for the present this is the northern terminus.
Opened	1 February 1913	
Closed	5 May 1941	
Reopened	1983 (resited)	
Operator original	LNWR	
current	PBR	

Opposite top right: The station is named after the nearby Whistle Inn public house, seen here on 5 June 2010 on the left-hand side immediately beyond the platform. It is famous for its collection of miners' lamps.

Main picture and below: Views of the station on 21 August 2010. *Both Terry Gough*

Maindee Loop   32, A2
(Maindee North Junction-Maindee East Junction)

New name (2011)	Hereford Loop	It is believed that the Loop was never formally closed to passenger trains, but just fell into disuse. It was, however, formally reinstated for passenger use in 1997, and until 2005 ten passenger trains per day were using it, including services between Penzance and the North West of England. It continues to be used by freight trains and is available as a diversionary route for passenger trains. It was singled in November 2010.
Opened	17 September 1874, initially freight only	
Closed	May 1970 to regular passenger trains (see below); has never closed to freight trains	
Reopened	late 1970s for occasional special trains, 27 July 1997 for regular passenger trains	
Closed	2005 to regular passenger trains	
Operator original	GWR	
current	NR	

Looking from North Junction towards South Junction on 6 June 2010. In the middle distance on the Loop can be seen the last vehicle of an eastbound freight from Deeside to Llanwern.

Cwmbran (Cwmbrân) 32, C1

Previous names	Pontnewydd, Lower Pontnewydd
Opened	21 December 1874
Closed	1 January 1917
Reopened	5 May 1919
Closed	9 June 1958
Reopened	12 May 1986 (resited)
Operator original	GWR
current	ATW

The original station of this name was on the Newport-Pontypool line and closed on 30 April 1962. The present station of Cwmbran is on the line between Newport and Pontypool Road (now called Pontypool & New Inn), and is just south of the site of Lower Pontnewydd station. The new station opened with investment from Mid Glamorgan County Council and Cwmbran Development Corporation at a cost of £215,000, with a 160-space car park, twin 135-yard platforms, footbridge, waiting shelters and ticket office. In the financial period 2007/8 the annual rail passenger usage was a quarter of a million. Currently Mondays to Saturdays there are one or two trains per hour in each direction, running between Cardiff Central/West Wales and Manchester Piccadilly, and interspersed with trains to Holyhead. On Sundays there is an hourly service.

Above: An overall view of the station on 8 August 1994, looking north towards Pontypool.

Right: No 158869 arrives as the 15.45 Cardiff Central to Manchester Piccadilly service on the same day.

USK AND WYE VALLEYS

Cefn Tilla Halt (32, B2)

Opened	14 June 1954	Between Llandenny and Usk, on the Pontypool Road to Ross-on-Wye line, this short-lived station was one of the smallest in the UK.
Closed	30 May 1955	
Operator	BR	

Cefn Tilla Halt is seen on 4 April 1955, just before closure, looking towards Pontypool Road. *Richard Casserley*

Hadnock Halt (32, B2)

Opened	7 May 1951	This single-platform halt between Symonds Yat and May Hill lasted only eight years, which, looking at its rural surrounds, is perhaps not too surprising. The nearest village is Dixton near Monmouth.
Closed	5 January 1959	
Operator	BR	

The site of Hadnock Halt, looking north on 21 March 2008. *Philip Halling*

Lydney Junction		32, B2
Opened	23 September 1875 (SWJR)	The former GWR station at Lydney Junction has never closed and is currently known as Lydney. It is a few minutes walk from the DFR station, which forms the southern terminus of the Dean Forest line. Services are provided throughout the year on most weekends and some weekdays, operated by diesel or steam power.
Resited	20 October 1879	
Closed	26 October 1960 (SWJR only)	
Reopened	1995	
P&PC	DFR Vol 1 pp6, 9-19, 114, Vol 2 pp34-46	
Operator original	GWR/SWJR	
current	DFR	

The wide island platform at Lydney Junction looking towards the connection with Network Rail on 14 April 2010.

St Mary's Halt   32, B2

Previous name	Lydney Lakeside	Between Lydney Junction and Lydney Town, the halt, a request stop, is named after the adjacent church. There is access to the station by footpath, and the single platform was rescued from Blaenrhondda.
Opened	8 September 1991	
P&PC	DFR Vol 1 pp20-21, 115, Vol 2 pp47-49	
Operator	DFR	

St Mary's Halt on 14 April 2010.

Lydney Town		32, B2
Opened	23 September 1875	The station is only a few minutes' walk from the town centre.
Closed	26 October 1964	
Reopened	April 2001	
P&PC	DFR Vol 1 pp22-31, Vol 2 pp50-52	
Operator original	SWJR	
current	DFR	

Above: Electro-diesel No E6001 works a train from Lydney Junction to Parkend on 14 April 2010.

Left: Looking along the platform towards Norchard.

Norchard		32, B2
Opened	1978, no train service	This is the home and administrative headquarters of the Dean Forest Railway, and includes the Norchard Steam Centre. It is not part of the original SWJR, but rather what remains of old colliery operations.
	1991, for service to Lydney Lakeside	
P&PC	DFR Vol 1 pp33-34, 118-121, Vol 2 pp54-56, 119-127	
Operator	DFR	

Above and right: Two views of the Low Level platform and yard looking north on 14 April 2010.

A train has just arrived at the High Level platform from Parkend on 14 April 2010. To the left is the Low Level platform.

Whitecroft (32, B2)

Opened	23 September 1875	In 2010 the station site was undergoing a complete reconstruction from scratch.
Closed	8 July 1929 (excursions to at least 1961)	
Reopened	2012 or later	
P&PC	DFR Vol 1 pp37-41, 122, Vol 2 pp59-63	
Operator original	SWJR	
current	DFR	

Part of the area to be developed at Whitecroft, seen on 3 December 1997 – the only platform at present proposed will be in its original position between the first and second telegraph poles on the left. *Brian Mills*

Parkend		32, B2
Previous name	Parkend Road	The station has two platforms, and the level crossing gates at the north end of the station are reputed to be the longest in Britain. This is currently the terminus of the DFR, but the railway is planning to extend further north.
Opened	23 September 1875	
Closed	8 July 1929 (excursion use in 1961)	
Reopened	26 December 2005	
P&PC	DFR Vol 1 pp 42-61, 123, 124, Vol 2 pp64-73	
Operator original	SWJR	
current	DFR	

Looking towards the end of the line on 14 April 2010 – there is a signal box on the left-hand side beyond the buildings near the crossing.

Kidderminster Town   41, B1

		Situated close to the London Midland main-line station of Kidderminster, it was called 'Town' to distinguish it and to follow GWR practice, where two stations existed, of giving the one nearest to the town centre the suffix 'Town'. The station was built from scratch, based on the GWR design for Ross-on-Wye station. The final wing was completed in 2006, with a canopy covering the station concourse. It is the southern terminus of the SVR.
Opened	July 1984	
P&PC	SVR p78	
Operator	SVR	

An interesting sounding brewer's van is being unloaded at the front of the station on 5 March 2010! There is a strong resemblance to Wrexham General station, with the 'French'-style ironwork.

Above: Class 2MT No 46443 has just been uncoupled from a train recently arrived from Bewdley on 5 March 2010.
On the left a Class 20 is stabled.

Below: An overall view of Kidderminster Town station on 14 March 1997, occupied by a solitary Class 50 diesel locomotive.

Bewdley 41, B1

Opened	1 February 1862
Closed	5 January 1970
Reopened	18 May 1974
P&PC	SVR pp4-5, 63-69, 94-95
Operator original	GWR
current	SVR

Situated on the line between Hartlebury and Shrewsbury, Bewdley became a junction station when the Tenbury & Bewdley Railway opened in 1864, then in 1878 the GWR opened a 'loop line' linking Bewdley with Kidderminster. Because of these circumstances, Bewdley has two signal boxes, North and South. Passenger traffic declined when the family car became established in the 1950s, although services hung on until early 1970. The station was disused for only four years before the new SVR bought the land, track and buildings, enabling it to extend from Bridgnorth. It was not until 1982, when the sugar beet traffic to Foley Park ended, and the opening of the SVR's own station at Kidderminster Town in 1984, that through services could be run the full length of the line.

Left: An overall view of the station from the footbridge, looking towards Kidderminster on 5 March 2010. On the left is ex-GWR tank engine No 6695 with a short goods train. The train on the island platform is awaiting departure for Kidderminster.

Below: Northwood Halt on 5 March 2010.

Northwood Halt 41, B1

Opened		17 June 1935
Closed		8 September 1963
Reopened		18 May 1974
P&PC		SVR p56
Operator	original	GWR
	current	SVR

This unstaffed request stop first opened in 1935, then closed and later reopened. It has a GWR-type 'Pagoda' waiting shelter on the platform.

Arley   41, B1

Opened	1 February 1862
Closed	9 September 1963
Reopened	18 May 1974
P&PC	SVR pp52-53
Operator original	GWR
current	SVR

A two-platform station with attractive buildings beautifully restored, it is situated just across the River Severn from the village of Upper Arley. It originally had a small goods yard, but after the cessation of the Alveley coal traffic the line became disused and the siding was removed, together with the station platforms, which were subsequently rebuilt.

The main station building is on the up platform, and beyond is the signal box,
as seen here looking towards Bridgnorth on 5 March 2010.

Highley		41, B1
Opened	1 February 1862	At one time Highley was a busy station, as there were four coal mines in the area, all connected by narrow- or standard-gauge branch lines. There were extensive sidings, but the freight workings ended in 1969 after the last colliery closure. However, the signal box survived, together with the station buildings; there is only one platform. From April 1974 to the middle of the following month Highley was the temporary southern terminus of the SVR. Today the very modern-looking 'Engine House' is only a short distance away to the south.
Closed	8 September 1963	
Reopened	13 April 1974	
P&PC	SVR pp49-51	
Operator original	GWR	
current	SVR	

Highley is a beautifully restored station in the best traditions of heritage railways.

Above: Highley's footbridge has only recently been installed.

The scene is enhanced by the arrival of a train headed by Class 5MT No 42968 on 25 October 2009.

Hampton Loade   41, B1

Opened	1 February 1862	Between 1970 and 1974 Hampton Loade was the southern terminus of the SVR, only 4½ miles from Bridgnorth. The station is fully manned and has two platforms, although when opened it only had one. The passing loop and second platform were added in 1983.
Closed	9 September 1963	
Reopened	23 May 1970	
P&PC	SVR pp46-47	
Operator original	GWR	
current	SVR	

Above: Standard 2-6-4T No 80079 arrives at the station from Bridgnorth on 23 July 1999.

left: A general view looking towards Bridgnorth, also on 23 July 1999.

Country Park Halt 41, B1

		An unmanned request stop with no highway access, the halt has a brick shelter but no other facilities. It was built on the site of Alveley Sidings, where a halt was provided for miners at the nearby colliery, which opened in 1937. The halt did not appear in the public timetable. The cost of the new station was met by Bridgnorth District Council as an access point to the Severn Valley Country Park.
Previous names	Alveley Halt, Alveley Colliery Halt, Alveley Sidings, Alveley Colliery Sidings	
Opened	1940	
Closed	9 September 1963	
Reopened	4 April 1996	
Operator original	GWR	
current	SVR	

Top: The down platform at Hampton Loade is seen on 25 October 2009, with the signal box at its far end.

Right: Country Park Halt on 25 October 2009.

Bridgnorth		41, B1
Opened	1 February 1862	Initially the main intermediate station of the Severn Valley line between Hartlebury and Shrewsbury, Bridgnorth subsequently became the northern terminus of the heritage line. The architecture of the station has been described as neo-Jacobean, and it is a listed building. There are two platforms and a substantial engine shed (the former Heaton Mersey diesel depot) close by the station.
Closed	8 September 1963	
Reopened	23 May 1970	
P&PC	SVR pp35-38	
Operator original	GWR	
current	SVR	

Right: A busy moment on 25 October 2009, with both platforms occupied. The signal box can be seen on the right-hand side beyond the building.

Below: Bridgnorth station, looking towards the end of the line on 23 July 1999.

The main entrance to Bridgnorth station.

Telford Central — 41, A1

Opened	12 May 1986	The station has twin platforms of intercity length, a substantial car park and excellent access to the nearby road system, including the M54 motorway. The cost was £700,000, funded jointly by British Rail, Telford Development Corporation and Shropshire County Council. Although the station was built to accommodate intercity trains to London Euston, these services no longer run. W&S operated trains to London Marylebone until 2011. The annual passenger usage remains pretty constant, from 2004/5 at 777,000 to 2007/8 at 799,000. There is currently a basically hourly service on Monday to Saturday, and approximately hourly from midday on Sunday.
Operator original	BR	
current	LM (also used by ATW)	

The modern station entrance with the town centre in the background, seen on 21 September 2009.

Above: This view, looking north, shows both platforms with the main buildings on the up side of the line.

Left: Looking south towards Wolverhampton.

Horsehay & Dawley   41,A1

Previous name	Horsehay
Opened	2 May 1859
Closed	23 July 1962
Reopened	May 1984
Closed	6 July 2011
Reopened	Expected early 2012
Operator original	GWR
current	TSR

The Telford Steam Railway is based at Horsehay & Dawley station and goods yard in Telford. The station was originally part of the GWR branch from Wellington to Craven Arms. Trains are run to a new terminus named Spring Village, and there are plans to extend the railway in both directions (see below).

Right: Horsehay & Dawley station on 26 May 2006. *Hugh Ballantyne*

Spring Village   41,A1

Opened	May 1984
Operator	TSR
Closed	6 July 2011
Reopened	Expected early 2012

Below: Rocket enters the station on 26 May 2006. *Hugh Ballantyne*

Lawley Common 41,A1

Previous name	Lawley Bank
Opened	2 May 1859
Closed	23 July 1962
Reopened	anticipated 2012 (resited)
Operator original	GWR
on reopening	TSR

Construction work on the station began in May 2009, and it will become the new northern terminus of the Telford Steam Railway

Doseley Halt (41,A1)

Opened	1 December 1932
Closed	23 July 1962
Reopened	anticipated 2012
Operator original	GWR
on reopening	TSR

This station lies south of Horsehay & Dawley and will become an intermediate station once the railway extends to Lightmoor Junction, where it will join the national network.

Above: Track-laying in progress at Lawley Common on 7 August 2010. *TSR*

Right: The site of Doseley Halt on 19 March 2006. *TSR*

Coalbrookdale (41,A1)

Other names	Telford (Coalbrookdale), Ironbridge Gorge	This station was located on the branch line from Madeley Junction to Ironbridge Power Station, which is used primarily for coal. The original station building is now used by the Green Wood Trust. In 1979 a temporary station, just north of the original, was built for visitors attending the bicentennial celebrations of the building of Ironbridge, and trains were run from Wolverhampton and other stations in the Midlands. The station was located adjacent to the Great Iron Warehouse, now the Coalbrookdale Museum of Iron. Eight years later the temporary station was reopened, and on this occasion services lasted for three years. The Telford Steam Railway hopes to be able to run trains on the line in the years to come.
Opened	1 November 1864	
Closed	23 July 1962	
Reopened	27 May 1979 (resited)	
Closed	2 September 1979	
Reopened	30 June 1987	
Closed	2 September 1990	
P&P	No 35 p36	
Operator original	GWR	
on closure	BR	

The first train arrives at the temporary station at Coalbrookdale on 27 May 1979. *Courtesy of Andrew Bannister*

Welshpool (Y Trallwng) 40, A1

Opened	14 August 1860	When the town by-pass was built, the old station was closed and a new one, consisting of an island platform, was constructed close by on a realignment. The old station building was originally the headquarters of the Oswestry & Newtown Railway (absorbed by the Cambrian Railways) and was built in the 'French Renaissance' style. Following closure it was converted for use as a craft centre. There is a service every 2 hours in each direction on Monday-Saturday (Birmingham International to Aberystwyth) and a reduced one on Sundays.
Closed	16 May 1992	
Reopened	18 May 1992 (resited)	
P&P	No 32 p83	
Operator original	CR/GWR	
current	ATW	

Above: This 5 February 1993 photograph was taken following the track deviation; the new station can be seen immediately beyond the footbridge.

Right: The new station, also looking east towards Shrewsbury, on 20 August 1993.

Llangollen — 51, C1

Opened	2 June 1862	
Closed	18 January 1965 (to passenger trains)	
Reopened	13 September 1975	
P&P	No 36 p97	
P&PC	*The Great Western in North Wales* pp17-22	
Operator original	GWR	
current	LlanR	

Situated close to the town centre and by the side of the River Dee, the station has two platforms with the main station buildings on the down side of the line. Trains run all year on most weekends and some weekdays; they are mostly steam-hauled, with some diesel locomotive and multiple unit workings. The service is currently provided between Llangollen and Carrog, and work on an extension to Corwen is well advanced.

The view from the road bridge over the River Dee. The photographs were taken on 17 September 2009.

Above: The east end of the line.

Beleow: Another shot from the road bridge, looking west.

Above: The view from platform level, also looking west.

Below: The west end of the station.

Ex-GWR Class 5600 0-6-2T No 5643 at Llangollen being admired at the head of a train to Carrog.

Berwyn	51, C1
Previous name	Berwyn Halt
Opened	8 May 1865
Closed	14 December 1964 (service suspended due to flood damage); 18 January 1965 (officially to passengers)
Reopened	19 October 1985
P&PC	*The Great Western in North Wales* pp24-25
Operator original	GWR
current	LlanR

The station has a single platform.

Berwyn station looking towards Llangollen on 23 October 2006.

0-6-0PT No 6430, masquerading as 'Duck', arrives at Berwyn from Carrog en route to Llangollen
on 17 September 2009. *P. D. Shannon*

Deeside Halt · 51, C1

Previous name	Dee-side
Opened	Easter weekend 1990 (services began), 16 June 1990 (officially)
Operator original	GWR
current	LlanR

Deeside Halt is a passing place, although trains stop on request. The halt was installed when the loop was the terminus of the Llangollen Railway, and allowed passengers to alight and watch the locomotive run round.

On 22 April 2007 we see the signal box (Deeside Loop), while on the platform can be seen a GWR-style 'Pagoda' waiting shelter.

Glyndyfrdwy · 51, C1

Opened	8 May 1865
Closed	14 December 1964 (prematurely: service suspended due to flood damage)
Reopened	1993
P&PC	*The Great Western in North Wales* pp26-28
Operator original	GWR
current	LlanR

The station is a passing place and has two platforms.

A view of the platforms, looking west on 17 September 2009.

There is a GWR-type 'Pagoda' building on the westbound platform at Glyndyfrdwy, and a signal box by the crossing gate at the Llangollen end of the station. The old box from Barmouth South has been erected at the Carrog end.

Carrog		50, C2
Opened	8 May 1865	There are two platforms with the main station buildings on the up side. Carrog remains the western terminus of the line until the final stretch to Corwen is reopened.
Closed	14 December 1964 (service suspended due to flood damage); 18 January 1965 (officially to passengers)	
Reopened	2 May 1996	
P&PC	*The Great Western in North Wales* pp4-5, 29-30	
Operator original	GWR	
current	LlanR	

Looking towards Llangollen on 17 September 2009.

Above: The station building at the west end.

Below: Looking west along the main platform.

0-6-0 pannier tank No 7754 has just arrived at Carrog from Llangollen on 11 April 2001.

Corwen		50, C2
Opened	8 May 1865	The Llangollen Railway is working on the 2½-mile extension from Carrog to Corwen, which will become the future terminus of the line. The original station site is not now accessible, so a new site has been acquired. The extension will be single-line, and the station will have a cantilevered platform in the GWR style, which will take eight coaches, and a run-round loop.
Closed	14 December 1964	
Reopened	anticipated March 2012 (resited)	
P&PC	*The Great Western in North Wales* pp32-35	
Operator original	GWR	
future	LlanR	

The site for the new station, seen here on 14 November 2010, is on part of the embankment (running across the photograph) that led to the old station, but closer to the town centre than the original and situated by the main town car park.

Inset: A ticket issued on 26 April 1956. *Terry Gough collection*

Wrexham Central (Wrecsam Canolog)   51, B1

Opened	1 November 1887	This is the terminus of the line from Bidston. In order to accommodate a new shopping centre, the old station was closed and a new one built 400 yards closer to General station; overnight the line was slewed into the new station and services continued! The line is promoted by the Borderlands Line Community Rail Partnership, and on Monday-Saturday there is an hourly service, reduced to five trains on Sundays starting mid-morning.
Closed	22 November 1998	
Reopened	23 November 1998 (resited)	
P&P	No 36 p91	
Operator original	CR	
current	ATW	

Top: The new station under construction on 27 Oct 1998. In the distance, in front of the church, the then existing Central station platform can just be seen.

Right: The completely new station is seen on 27 October 1999, with the church still visible.

Above: A ticket issued on 20 October 1958. *Terry Gough collection*

Above: Class 142 No 142043 awaits departure to Bidston on the same day.

Below: The very modern new-style station frontage on 5 September 2007.

Glan Conwy   50, A1

Previous names	Llansaintffraidd, Glan Conway
Opened	17 June 1863
Closed	26 October 1964
Reopened	4 May 1970
Operator original	LNWR
current	ATW

The station, which is a request stop, is situated in the centre of Llansantffraid village, between Llandudno Junction and Tal-y-Cafn on the branch line to Blaenau Ffestiniog, which is promoted by the Conwy Valley Rail Initiative. The station buildings are in private hands. In the 2007/8 financial year the passenger usage was less than 3,000, a reduction from 2004/5 when it was not far short of 5,000. Currently on Mondays to Saturdays there are six trains per day in each direction, including two starting at Llandudno Junction rather than Llandudno. There are only three trains on Sundays until September, when they are replaced by buses. The branch is prone to flooding.

Dolgarrog   50, B1

Opened	18 December 1916
Closed	26 October 1964
Reopened	14 June 1965
Operator original	LNWR
current	ATW

There were adjacent sidings and an interchange facility with the short standard-gauge industrial line, approximately 1½ miles long, serving the village and the aluminium works, which closed in 1960. In 2007/8 passenger usage was less than 1,000. There are five trains a day Monday-Saturday, including two starting at Llandudno Junction, and three a day on Sundays, including one from Llandudno Junction, until September, when they are replaced by buses for the winter; this arrangement applies to all stations on the branch.

Above: Looking from Glan Conwy towards Llandudno Junction on 5 March 1994, we see the old station house on the platform.

Below: The modest platform and waiting shelter at Dolgarrog, looking towards Llanrwst on 5 March 1994.

Llanrwst 50, B1

Opened:		29 July 1989
Operator	original	BR
	current	ATW

Built primarily to bring the railway closer to the town centre, this new station in a new position resulted in the renaming of the existing Llanrwst to Llanrwst North. The annual passenger usage in the financial year 2007/8 was just over 14,500.

Left: Llanrwst station, looking towards Blaenau Ffestiniog on 5 March 1994.

Below: Class 101 unit No 101677 forms the 11.45 service to Llandudno at Blaenau Ffestiniog on 4 May 2000.

Blaenau Ffestiniog 50, C1

Previous name	Blaenau Ffestiniog Central
Opened	10 September 1883
Closed	4 January 1960
Reopened	22 March 1982 (delayed by bad weather)
P&P	No 36 pp108-109
P&PC	*The Great Western in North Wales* pp91-95
Operator original	GWR
current	ATW

Blaenau Ffestiniog is the terminus of the branch from Llandudno Junction and is a joint station with the narrow gauge Ffestiniog Railway. The current station was built on the site of the old GWR Central station, having attracted close to £1 million of investment from the Welsh Agency, the local authority and a European fund. Beyond the station the line continues to Trawsfynydd, and until 1995 was used for carrying nuclear flasks to and from the power station. The annual ATW passenger usage in the 2007/8 financial year was 36,500, well ahead of previous years.

Above: The same unit is seen departing, with activity on the Ffestiniog Railway on the right, which runs to Porthmadog.

Below: Diesel unit No 150280 has just arrived from Llandudno on 26 June 2007.

Maentwrog Road   50, C1

Opened	1 November 1882
Closed	4 January 1960
Reopened	23 July 1989, as Trawsfynydd, for visitors to lake
Closed	10 September 1989
Reopening	2011 proposed
P&P	No 36 p107
P&PC	*The Great Western in North Wales* p87
Operator original	GWR
at closure	BR

One of the seven intermediate stations between Bala and Blaenau Ffestiniog, it served the villages of Gellilydan, Maentwrog and Tanybwlch, the latter being 3 miles away! During the temporary opening from July to September 1989, two public passenger trains ran each day from Blaenau Ffestiniog through Maentwrog Road (renamed Trawsfynydd) almost to the end of the line at Trawsfynydd Power Station. Until the closure of the power station and disposal of nuclear waste the branch line was in regular use by loaded flask traffic being taken to Llandudno Junction for onward movement to Sellafield. The line closed completely in 1998. The station building is in private hands, but there are plans to reopen the line between Blaenau Ffestiniog and Trawsfynydd as a heritage railway, with trains linking to boat cruises on Trawsfynydd Lake.

Above: The single line looking towards Trawsfynydd on 5 March 1994.

Right: The station house was photographed on the same day, with a sign advertising that it was in use as an organic nursery business.

Shotton		51, B1
Previous name	Shotton Low Level	The station, between Conwy and Flint, was reopened to create an interchange with the High Level platforms on the Wrexham Central to Bidston line, later known as the Borderlands Line. There is mainly an hourly service in each direction on Monday-Saturday (between Llandudno and Manchester Piccadilly), and on Sundays there is one train before midday, then hourly.
Opened	1 April 1907	
Closed	14 February 1966	
Reopened	21 August 1972	
Operator original	LNWR	
current	ATW	

Looking north towards Flint on 19 July 1994, Class 156 No 156426 departs for the North Wales coast.

In this view from the down platform looking towards Chester on 4 June 1993, a four-car unit with No 158749 at the rear forms a Manchester Piccadilly service.

The station was refurbished during 2010, as seen in this 14 November photograph.

Conwy   50, A1

Previous name	Conway
Opened	1 May 1848
Closed	14 February 1966
Reopened	29 June 1987
P&P	No 36 pp36-37
Operator original	LNWR
current	ATW

Between Llandudno Junction and Penmaenmawr, the station is located within the walls of Conwy Castle and the platforms can take four-car trains. Funding of £267,000 came from Gwynedd County Council and the Welsh Office. Passenger usage show an increase from the 18,500 of 2004/5 to 26,000 in 2007/8. It is a request stop for all trains, and currently on Monday-Saturday the service is basically one train per hour, while on Sundays there is an irregular service of nine trains in total. Services are from Crewe, Birmingham New Street or Cardiff Central and terminate at Holyhead.

Class 37 No 37421 (in EWS livery) passes through the station with the 12.51 Holyhead to Crewe service on 28 March 2000.

The view looking in the Holyhead direction on the same day.

Llanfairpwll 49, A2

Previous name	Llanfair PG
Opened	1 August 1848
Closed	14 February 1966
Reopened	29 May 1970 as Llanfair PG, temporary terminus
Closed	31 January 1972
Reopened	7 May 1973
Operator original	LNWR
current	ATW

The station has the longest name in Britain, but the platforms are very short, at 40 yards. It was used as a terminus for trains from the mainland after the fire on the Britannia Bridge. It is a request stop, and the annual passenger usage shows a considerable increase from 6,000 in 2004/5 to virtually double that number in 2007/8. In the summer of 2011 the Monday-Saturday service was irregular, comprising eight services in all, with an irregular service of seven trains in total on Sundays. All up services originate at Holyhead, and destinations include Chester, Manchester Piccadilly, Birmingham New Street and Cardiff Central.

A platform ticket issued by BR in the late 1950s. *Terry Gough collection*

Left: A three-car Class 101 diesel unit enters the station with the 15.13 Holyhead-Llandudno Junction service on 10 June 1990.

Below: Travelling in the other direction on 26 March 1997, another 'Heritage' Class 101 unit (No 101685) in green livery heads for the mainland and Llandudno. Llanfair PG crossing box can just be seen beyond the front of the unit.

The main station building at Llanfairpwll, seen here on 19 July 1995, is situated on the up side, and was renovated by Edinburgh Woollen Mills, which has a retail outlet close by. Part of the station building is a railway museum.

Valley (Y Dyffryn, or Y Fali)   49, A1

Opened	May or June 1849	The station was reopened with the help of a grant of £15,000 from Gwynedd County Council, Ynys Mon Borough and four Community Councils. The station building was designed by Francis Thompson. There are road-to-rail transfer sidings nearby for the dispatch of spent fuel from Wylfa nuclear power station. Annual usage in 2007/8 was approaching 19,000. Currently on Mondays to Saturdays the service is irregular, comprising nine services in all, with an irregular service of six trains in total on Sundays. Services run between Holyhead and several cities, including Chester, Cardiff and Birmingham. It is a request stop.
Closed	14 February 1966	
Reopened	15 March 1982	
Operator original	LNWR	
current	ATW	

This was the view on 22 June 1993, looking towards Holyhead from the crossing, which is protected by the semaphore signal on the right.

Birchwood 52, A1

Opened	6 October 1980
Operator original	BR
current	FTPE

Located between Glazebrook and Padgate and close to the main Birchwood shopping complex, the station has twin platforms 228 yards long, modern station buildings, a covered footbridge and car park. The cost of £445,000 was jointly funded by BR, Warrington New Town and Cheshire County Council. In 2007/8 the passenger usage was approaching half a million. Train services are currently hourly seven days a week from Liverpool Lime Street to Newcastle/Hull/Scarborough by FTPE. Services from Warrington Central to Manchester Oxford Road are operated by Northern, and a few trains to Norwich by EMT.

Looking towards Liverpool Lime Street on 7 August 2009, the main station building is on the opposite (eastbound) platform.

Another view of the station, looking east.

Halewood 51, A2

		Situated in south Liverpool in the metropolitan borough of Knowsley, the station was built at a cost of £440,000 to serve a 10,000 catchment area within a half-mile radius. There is a ticket office at street level, with ramps leading to the platforms, which have brick shelters. In the financial year 2007/8 passenger usage was more than 50,000. Services run between Liverpool to the west and Manchester to the east, and comprise one or two trains per hour in each direction on Monday to Saturday, and hourly on Sunday.;
Opened	May 1874	
Closed	17 September 1951	
Reopened	16 May 1988 (new station)	
Operator original	CLC	
current	Northern	

Class 156 No 156497 leaves Halewood for Liverpool on 9 September 2009.

Liverpool Central (Deep Level) 59, B1

		The station was built with one platform on the single loop-line tunnel for Wirral trains that links James Street with Moorfields, Lime Street and Central stations. Between Hunts Cross and Southport trains run every few minutes on Monday to Saturday, with two services per hour on Sunday. Between Moorfields and New Brighton, West Kirby, Ellesmere Port and Chester there are trains every few minutes on Monday to Saturday, and each service has two trains per hour on Sunday.
Opened	9 May 1977	
Operator original	Merseyrail Electrics	
current	Merseyrail	

The three destinations of West Kirby, Ellesmere Port and New Brighton are shown on the train information screen as unit No 507030 enters the station on 9 September 2009.

Brunswick   59, C2

		Located south of Liverpool Central on the 'Northern' line, this is a modern station close to the business park, in the Dingle area of the city; at one time there was an engine shed close by in a deep cutting, which filled the atmosphere with steam and smoke. The station cost £3 million with contributions from Merseyside Development Corporation and Urban Regeneration Grants. Trains run in each direction (between Hunts Cross and Southport) four times an hour on Monday-Saturday, and twice an hour on Sundays. In 2007/8 the annual passenger usage was more than 400,000.
Opened	26 March 1998	
P&P	No 39 pp37-39	
Operator original	Merseyrail Electrics	
current	Merseyrail	

Left: The plaque commemorating the opening of the station.

Below: The station entrance.

Above: The modern booking office.

Below: Looking towards Liverpool, unit No 508112 enters the station. All photos at Brunswick taken on 9 September 2009..

St Michaels	59, C2
Opened	1 June 1864
Closed	17 April 1972
Reopened	3 January 1978
Operator original	CLC
current	Merseyrail

The main station building is at street level, spanning the lines in a cutting. When reopened the cost was part funded by Marks & Spencer plc, because of the company's use of the 'St Michael' brand. A well-used station following the Liverpool Garden Festival in 1984, in the financial period 2007/8 the annual passenger usage was nearly 340,000. There are four trains an hour on Mondays to Saturdays to Southport via Liverpool Central to the north and Hunts Cross to the south; on Sundays trains are two an hour in each direction.

Above: Trains cross at St Michaels on 9 September 2009, No 507027 on the left and No 507001 on the right, seen from the street-level entrance.

Below: The station entrance.

Aigburth   59, C2

Previous names	Mersey Road, Mersey Road & Aigburth	The station lies between Cressington and St Michaels. In 2007/8 the annual passenger usage was more than a quarter of a million. Trains operate four times an hour on Mondays to Saturdays, reduced to two on Sundays, in each direction between Hunts Cross and Southport.
Opened	1 June 1864	
Closed	17 April 1972	
Reopened	3 January 1978	
P&P	No 39 p36	
Operator original	CLC	
current	Merseyrail	

The main building seen from platform level on 8 October 2009.

A view of the station building across the footbridge.

Cressington   59, C2

Previous name	Cressington & Grassendale
Opened	April 1872
Closed	17 April 1972
Reopened	3 January 1978
Operator original	CLC
current	Merseyrail

The station serves the Grassendale district of Liverpool, the name of Cressington being taken from the nearby Cressington Park. It is a Grade II listed building, for its traditional façade. As part of the Merseyrail upgrade, the platforms were lengthened to accommodate six-car trains, but this created a problem as the station is between two bridges in a narrow cutting. Special dispensation was granted by the Railway Inspectorate to build part of the platforms narrower than the normal width of 6 feet. In 2007/8 annual passenger usage was 165,000. On Mondays to Saturdays there are four trains an hour in each direction (Southport to the north and Hunts Cross to the south), reduced to two on Sundays.

This is the street-level entrance to the station on 8 October 2009, providing an interesting view of the 'fairy castle' effect of the chimneys.

The main building on the Hunts Cross platform.

Liverpool South Parkway   51,A2

Previous names	Allerton, Garston
Opened	15 February 1864 (Allerton); 1 April 1874 (Garston)
Closed	1 August 2005 (Allerton); 11 June 2006 (Garston)
Reopened	11 June 2006
Operator original	LNWR/CLC
current	Merseyrail (lower platforms; other platforms used by EMT, LM and Northern)

As can be seen from the photographs, this is a very modern station, situated in Garston and built as a bus/rail interchange for Liverpool John Lennon Airport. The construction cost £32 million, which was about double the original forecast. The main-line platforms are on the site of the former Allerton station, which closed in 2005 to allow the rebuilding work to proceed. The Northern line platforms are completely new, built at a lower level, and replace Garston station, which was slightly to the west of the new station. There are six platforms in all, a substantial car park and bus station. In 2009 ticket barriers were introduced at both ends of the concourse. In 2008/9 the annual passenger usage was more than half a million. On the Northern line, Mondays to Saturdays, there are four trains per hour to Southport in the north and Hunts Cross in the south, and two per hour on Sundays. On the higher-level platforms there are five or six trains per hour in each direction on the City line between Liverpool Lime Street and Warrington Central (from various departure points), then one to four trains per hour on Sundays. The EMT service is between Liverpool and Nottingham/Norwich, and LM between Liverpool and Birmingham New Street

The exterior of the station on 7 August 2009.

No 350240 works a Birmingham to Lime Street service on 9 September 2009.

Above: At the lower level No 508141 forms a southbound service on 9 September 2009.

Below: On 7 August 2009 No 156488 departs from Liverpool South Parkway for Lime Street with a service from Birmingham.

Conway Park		59, B1
Opened	22 June 1998	Situated between Birkenhead Hamilton Square and Birkenhead Park, twin 144-yard platforms, with escalators, lifts, booking hall and other facilities, were provided for the £15.7-million 'underground' station, serving the town centre of Birkenhead. The rail service is every few minutes on Monday to Saturday and four trains per hour on Sunday in each direction, with destinations on the Wirral of New Brighton and West Kirby.
Operator original	Merseyrail Electrics	
current	Merseyrail	

Left: The entrance to the station features a rather unusual canopy, photographed on 27 January 2000.

Below: Conway Park 'underground' station, serving Birkenhead town centre, is seen on 9 September 2009.

Bromborough Rake 51,A1

Opened	30 September 1985
Operator original	BR
current	Merseyrail

This is one of two new stations serving the Bromborough area of the Wirral. The word 'Rake' appears to have two definitions, probably dating back to a Viking past – one is simply 'Lane' and the other meaning is 'to drive', as in herding sheep. The word also appears in the title of Eastham station. The station cost £200,000, which was met by Merseyside PTE with the assistance of a European grant. In the financial period 2007/8 annual passenger usage was more than 141,000. In the summer of 2011 there was a train every few minutes on Monday to Saturday, and four trains per hour on Sunday, to and from Liverpool.

Left: The modern entrance and booking office, photographed on 4 September 2009.

Below: The view towards Birkenhead at platform level.

Eastham Rake   51, A1

		Built primarily to serve the village of Eastham, the station cost £2 million, which was funded by Merseyside PTE. Currently there is a service every few minutes on Monday to Saturday, and four trains per hour on Sunday, to and from Liverpool Central. In the last four financial periods the annual passenger figures have risen from 131,000 to 171,000.
Opened	3 April 1995	
Operator original	Merseyrail Electrics	
current	Merseyrail	

Left: The modern entrance and ticket office on 4 September 2009.

Below: The view along the platform towards Bromborough.

Overpool 51,A1

Opened	16 August 1988
Operator original	BR
current	Merseyrail

The twin six-car platforms cost £263,000, funded by £193,000 from Cheshire County Council and the balance from Merseyside PTE. The station is situated close to Ellesmere Port, and saw nearly 34,000 passengers in the financial period 2007/8. There is a half-hourly service seven days a week between Ellesmere Port and Liverpool Central.

The view towards Eastham Rake on 18 August 2009 shows the basic station platforms.

Runcorn East 51,A2

Previous name	Norton
Opened	circa March 1852
Closed	1 September 1952
Reopened	3 October 1983
Operator original	LNWR
current	ATW

Built just to the south west of the original Norton station, and opened to serve new housing estates, the station provides twin platforms of eight-coach length, ticket office, waiting shelters, car parking, lighting and a ramped footbridge. It cost £385,000, with contributions of £100,000 each from Cheshire County Council and Warrington Development Corporation, the balance covered by British Rail. A 30% grant was also received from the European Commission. The annual passenger usage has increased from 108,000 in 2004/5 to nearly 120,000 in 2007/8. There is an hourly service seven days a week from Manchester Piccadilly to Llandudno.

This is the view looking towards Warrington on 4 September 2009. The signal box, which can be seen at the end of the westbound platform, still carries the name of the old station of Norton.

On 18 August 1990 Class 47 No 47479 heads through Runcorn East with an empty parcels train from Holyhead to Manchester Red Bank, passing under the station footbridge with the booking office just visible on the right.

Moorfields (Low and Deep Level Platforms) 59, B1

Opened	2 May 1977 (Low level) 8 May 1978 (Deep Level	This is one of the three stations on the one-way underground system in central Liverpool, the others being Lime Street and Central. Moorfields acts as an interchange with the Northern line (Southport/ Ormskirk to Hunts Cross) and the Wirral line. There are three platforms, one of which – serving the Wirral line – is at a much deeper level, because the Northern line tunnels pass over Queensway while the Wirral line passes beneath it. There is a service every few minutes seven days a week. The station is normally quieter at the weekends, as it is primarily used by workers in the city centre.
Operator original	Merseyrail Electrics	
current	Merseyrail	

The entrance to the station on Moorfields, Liverpool (between Tithebarn Street and Dale Street), on 8 October 2009.

The Deep Level platform at Moorfields for trains to the Wirral, photographed on 9 September 2009.

Liverpool Lime Street (Deep Level) — 59, B1

Opened	30 October 1977	Situated under Liverpool's main-line terminus of the same name, this loop-line station carries trains running clockwise from and back to the Wirral – New Brighton, West Kirby, Ellesmere Port and Chester. The station at deep level consists of a single platform and is connected to the main-line station by a pedestrian subway and escalators. The Wirral line trains operate every 5 minutes Monday-Saturday, and with a 5- and 10-minute frequency on Sundays.
Operator original	Merseyrail Electrics	
current	Merseyrail	

No 507010 awaits departure on the Wirral line on 9 September 2009.

Wavertree Technology Park   59, B2

		This modern new station was a £2-million project, built primarily to serve the new business park, as its name implies. It has a frequent seven-day-a-week service in each direction, and the annual passenger usage has risen to more than 200,000 in the financial period 2007/8. Services run between Liverpool Lime Street and Wigan North Western and Manchester Airport; there are frequent services on Monday to Saturday, and two trains per hour on Sunday.
Opened	13 August 2000	
Operator original	FNW	
current	Merseyrail	

The booking office is located on the modern footbridge, photographed on 9 September 2009.

Whiston		51,A2
Opened	1 October 1990	Situated between Rainhill and Huyton, the station consists of two 119-yard platforms with basic facilities; it cost £420,000, which was shared between Merseyside PTE and Knowsley Borough Council. The annual passenger figure for the financial period 2007/28 was approaching 150,000. On Monday-Saturday there are two trains per hour to Manchester Victoria and Warrington Bank Quay. On Sundays the service is basically hourly.
Operator original	BR	
current	Northern	

Above: The platforms at Whiston on 9 September 2009.

Below: The entrance to the station on the down side of the line.

Index of locations